High Voice

15 EASY CHRISTMAS CAROL ARRANGEMENTS

FOR THE PROGRESSING SINGER

EDITED BY RICHARD WALTERS

To access companion recorded full performances
and piano accompaniments online, visit:
www.halleonard.com/mylibrary

Enter Code
5365-7396-7008-0260

ISBN 978-1-4234-1336-3

7777 W. BLUEMOUND RD. P.O. BOX 13819 MILWAUKEE, WI 53213

Visit Hal Leonard Online at
www.halleonard.com

In Australia Contact:
Hal Leonard Australia Pty. Ltd.
4 Lentara Court
Cheltenham, Victoria, 3192 Australia
Email: ausadmin@halleonard.com.au

CONTENTS

Singers on the recordings: *Tanya Kruse, soprano; **Steven Stolen, tenor

Pianists on the recordings: †Brian Dean
                             ††Christopher Ruck
                             †††Richard Walters

PREFACE

The recent collections for singers, *15 Easy Folksong Arrangements* and *15 Easy Spiritual Arrangements*, published in 2004 and 2005, have been met with enthusiasm, as I predicted they would when I prepared prefaces for both volumes. Richard Walters has now introduced this new addition to the series, *15 Easy Christmas Carol Arrangements*, and I am again pleased to answer his request to write a preface.

My compilation *Christmas Solos for All Ages*, with 45 songs in High, Medium and Low Voice editions, is a general use collection for older teens, college and adult students. In contrast, *15 Easy Christmas Carol Arrangements* is for singers of any age with less experience, those in the first year or two of study. The vocal ranges are modest. The High Voice volume does not go above an F, and even that note is rare. The Low Voice key has a particularly low tessitura, rarely going above a C. The arrangements are for an inexperienced singer to remain comfortably in a middle to lower-middle tessitura.

Christmas is always a fun time for my students (those who have no religious objections) to be given several interesting seasonal solos to learn each year. The songs are familiar, melodious, relatively easy, and add a different dimension to the usual studio repertoire. Of course, these carol arrangements can be used in church services or community Christmas events. Many public schools no longer accept our vast genre of lovely Christmas carols with a religious theme for their December programs, but this depends on the community. You should find out from your local middle school and high school teachers if Christmas solos are used in their programs. Private schools, depending on their nature, and parochial schools may be more accepting.

The selection of songs includes very familiar carols, such as "The First Noel," "Away in a Manger," and "Silent Night," plus some lesser known beautiful gems like "Once in Royal David's City," "Coventry Carol" and "Infant Holy, Infant Lowly." The most unusual carol for Americans is the very singable yet unfamiliar British melody of "It Came upon the Midnight Clear."

The accompaniments are designed for intermediate pianists, yet they have a distinct, contemporary flavor. These carols will help introduce singers and pianists to a fresh, modern style of arrangements that I think most, especially the young, will find appealing. The recordings feature professional singers, illustrating one model of interpretation, and an accompaniment track for practice, and in some studios, in lessons. I always caution that teachers need to guide a student's use of the recordings as practice tools. It should be used for musical guidance, but students should not attempt to imitate the vocal tone of the recorded performers.

This book provides a wonderful introduction to solo Christmas music for a singer's seasonal use. I can even envision groups of these selections performed by adult singers, as several of my adult students have done with the folksongs and spirituals volumes.

Joan Frey Boytim
May, 2006

ABOUT THE CAROLS . . .

AWAY IN A MANGER

This American carol, possibly of Pennsylvania German Lutheran origin, has a muddled history. It first appeared in print in 1887 in a collection of carols edited by James Ramsey Murray, who was possibly the composer of the original melody. The author of the verses is unknown, though for several decades this carol was mistakenly attributed to Martin Luther. The carol has appeared in many different musical versions. Printed in this volume is the "Cradle Song" melody composed by William J. Kirkpatrick (1838–1921).

COVENTRY CAROL

This English lullaby is one of the few Christmas carols that tells the story of Herod's slaughter of the innocents. We hear the lament of mothers that mourn the loss of their young sons. The words come from *The Pageant of the Shearman and the Tailors*, one of the many popular mystery plays produced in the English city of Coventry in the 15th century. Unfortunately, the original manuscripts of both the music and the poetry have been lost. Robert Croo (d. 1534) has been credited with writing the words as we know them today. The melody was found and preserved by Thomas Sharp (1770–1841), published in *A Dissertation on the Pageants, or Dramatic Mysteries, Anciently Performed at Coventry*, 1825.

THE FIRST NOEL

First published in William Sandys' *Christmas Carols, Ancient and Modern* (England, 1833), "The First Noel" is one of the oldest and most popular carols in the English language. Both the words and music are anonymous and scholars disagree as to whether this carol originates from England or France. The Old English title uses the word "nowell." It may have come from the French "noël" and "nouvelle," or the Latin "novella" and "natilis," all words associated with newness and birth.

GOOD CHRISTIAN FRIENDS, REJOICE

This is the 14th century German melody "In dulci jubilo." The original text in Latin is attributed to Heinrich Suso (c.1295–1366). According to folklore, Suso, a Dominican minister and a mystic, heard angels sing these words, and after dancing with them, penned the melody and text. The text was later freely translated into English by John Mason Neale, and first appeared in *Carols for Christmastide* in London in 1853. Neale also authored texts to "O Come, O Come Emmanuel" and "Good King Wenceslas." The carol is presented here in an inclusive, gender-neutral adaptation, adopted by several present-day hymnals (rather than the original "Good Christian Men, Rejoice").

HE IS BORN

The text of this French carol, "Il est né, le divin enfant," appears in many translations, including "He Is Born, the Holy Child" and "Born Is He, Little Child Divine." The tune first appeared in R. Gosjean's *Airs des noêl lorrain* (1862), where it is called "Ancient air de chasse." It is melodically very similar to an old Normandy hunting tune "Le tête bizarde" (The Bizzare Head). The text of the carol was first published in Geoffrey Brace's *Noêls anciens* (1875–6). Most likely the text and music were put together in the 18th century, mimicking a rustic style and bagpipe drone.

IN THE BLEAK MIDWINTER

The words of this English carol are by Christina Georgina Rossetti (1830–1894). Born to Italian immigrants in England, Rossetti was a devout Anglican, which profoundly influenced most of her three books of poetry and four books of devotions. She is associated with the Pre-Raphaelite movement, in part founded by her two brothers. For the 1906 *English Hymnal*, Gustav Holst (1874–1934) wrote a hymn setting "Cranham" of Rossetti's poetry.

INFANT HOLY, INFANT LOWLY

The first significant Polish carol, it first appeared during the 13th or 14th centuries. The text has appeared in several different English translations, such as "Jesus Holy, Born So Lowly" and "Baby Jesus, in a Manger." The translation presented here is by Edith Margaret Gellibrand Reed (1885–1933).

IT CAME UPON THE MIDNIGHT CLEAR

Edmund Hamilton Sears (1810–1876) spent most of his life in the small towns of the rural Berkshire Hills of Massachusetts. He attended Union College and Harvard Divinity School before his work as a Unitarian minister in the small towns of Weston, Wayland and Lancaster. The poem was first published in the *Christian Register* in 1849. There is a famous setting of the poem which uses the melody from "Carol" (1850) composed by Richard Storrs Willis (1819–1900). In this publication, we have chosen the setting by Arthur Sullivan, the standard British version of the carol. This tune is an arrangement of the traditional air "Noel." Sullivan's version was published in *Church Hymns with Tunes* (1874).

JOSEPH, DEAREST JOSEPH MINE

The German words of this carol are originally "Josef, Lieber Josef Mein," dating from the 14th or 15th century. The text was used in a mystery play, a medieval form of drama that centered around the nativity. These plays were first performed in advent church services, but later moved into the secular realm. The tune of this carol, "Resonet in Laudibus" (Let our praises resound) is most likely from the 14th century or earlier. While not devoid of Marian imagery, this carol is unique for its attention to Joseph. The melody has been used by many composers over the years, including Orlando de Lassus, Jacob Handl, and notably in "Geistliches Wiegenlied" by Johannes Brahms.

O COME, LITTLE CHILDREN

Christoph von Schmid (1768–1854), a German Roman Catholic priest and schoolmaster, wrote a vast amount of literature for children. Around 1850, near the end of his life, Schmid wrote the words to "Ihr Kindlein, kommet" ("O Come, Little Children"). The carol was set to an existing melody by the composer, conductor, organist Johann Abraham Peter Schulz (1747–1800). In this carol, all young children are called to worship the baby Jesus.

O COME, O COME EMMANUEL

The origins of the tune possibly lie in the Roman Catholic plainsong service music of the 12th or 13th centuries, but maybe even as early as Charlemagne (771–814). The seven Latin antiphons that make up the text are sung at vespers in the seven days of advent that proceed Christmas. They are often referred to as the "O Antiphons" because they all start with "O": *O Sapentia* (O Wisdom), *O Adonai* (O Lord), *O Radix Jesse* (O Root of Jesse), etc. These were plainsong chants in Gregorian mode. In 1851, John Mason Neale (1818–1866), an English clergyman, translated five of the antiphons into English, adapting the ancient melody as well to make the basis of the carol.

ONCE IN ROYAL DAVID'S CITY

Written in 1848 by Mrs. Cecil Frances Alexander (formerly Fanny Humphreys), this hymn was composed with simple lyrics so that young children may understand its message. Mrs. Alexander (1823–1895) taught Sunday school in her native Ireland and, over the course of her life, wrote many hymns and poems for both children and adults. Some of her more popular hymns include "All Things Bright and Beautiful" and "Jesus Calls Us." This hymn text was first published in the 1848 collection *Hymns for Little Children*. In 1849 it was set to music by the organist and organ designer Henry J. Gauntlett, a prolific composer of hymns. It is rumored that he composed over 10,000. Among his admirers was Mendelssohn, who praised his literary accomplishments as well as his vast knowledge of music history. Having difficulty grasping their catechism, it is said that Mrs. Alexander wrote this hymn to help her godchildren better understand the story of Jesus' birth.

SILENT NIGHT

The folklore about the origins of this carol is nearly as well known as the carol itself. While a definitive history of the carol is impossible to ascertain, the traditional story tells of the Rev. Joseph Mohr, the assistant clergy at St. Nicholas Church in Oberndorf, Austria, and Franz Xaver Grüber, deputy organist at the same parish. Mohr penned the verses to "Silent Night" for use during the Midnight Mass on Christmas Eve, 1818. Grüber wrote the music for two solo voices with choir and guitar accompaniment, the organ being in disrepair. The carol passed orally throughout Austria, and eventually was heard in the United States in 1839. The words were translated into its best-known English version in 1863 by John Freeman Young (1820–1885), an Episcopal Bishop.

STILL, STILL, STILL

Both the tune and the lyrics of this gentle lullaby are anonymous. It is either of German or Austrian origin. The original German title is *Stille, Stille, Stille*. There have been many versions of lyrics for this carol in English translation. With different lyrics, this song has been used as a lullaby year round.

SUSSEX CAROL

This carol first appeared in 1684 in the volume *A Small Garland of Pious and Godly Songs* published by Luke Wadding, an Irish bishop. It is unknown whether Wadding was the original composer. The carol is named for the region of origin in England. A true English folksong, the carol was collected in Sussex in 1904 by Ralph Vaughan Williams and Cecil Sharp. It was first titled "Another Short Carol for Christmas Day" and is also known as "On Christmas Night," or "On Christmas Night All Christians Sing." Vaughan Williams published a harmonized, hymnal-style version of the carol in 1919, commonly sung today.

ABOUT THE RECORDINGS
AND ARRANGEMENTS

Even though this material is designed primarily for first and second year voice students, we deliberately chose to record the performances with professional singers at a high level of development, rather than recording young, student voices. Hearing a real singer phrase and express a piece of music is excellent instruction. It also may inspire you, and fire your imagination.

A gifted singer has vibrato in his or her voice naturally. It is part of the color of an individual voice. Instrumentalists sometimes do not understand this, because wind and string players have to work at learning how to create vibrato in their playing, which is actually an imitation of singing. In your choral experience as a singer a director may have asked specifically for a "pure tone" without vibrato at times. But for solo classical singing, and for those in traditional voice lessons, vibrato is a natural part of opening up the voice. This is important to understand for those young or inexperienced persons just becoming familiar with classical singing. The singers on the recordings are doing nothing deliberate regarding vibrato. They are just singing in a healthy, supported manner with their natural vocal sound, just as you should do with your own voice.

We urge you not to imitate the performers on the recordings. Do not attempt to imitate their tone or the details of their performances. These recordings are for familiarizing you with the songs and arrangements. It is very important for you to come up with your own interpretation. You can only do this after you know the song very well, and have experimented with different ways of phrasing, worked on diction, and pondered the words of a song. Your teacher will undoubtedly help you with interpretation.

We necessarily must choose one tempo in recording a piano accompaniment track for you to use in your practice. Our choice of tempo, phrasing, *ritardandos*, and dynamics is carefully considered, usually played by the arranger himself in the case of *15 Easy Christmas Carol Arrangements*. But by the nature of recording, it is only one choice. You may find in working with a pianist that you need a slightly faster or slower tempo than on the recordings, and you also may have your own interpretive ideas that differ from our recordings.

Companion recordings such as this are best used with the guidance of a voice teacher, who can help point out to you things you may need to do to accommodate your voice and singing.

These carol arrangements were created with the progressing voice in mind. The ranges are modest, as are the musical issues addressed. We tried to treat this work more as organic composition, with all the values of full composition, rather than an approach to arranging that harmonizes a melody. The accompaniments should be accessible to intermediate student pianists.

We aimed to create useful and expressive arrangements that will hold up as musically substantial even for more experienced singers. Our wish is that you may inspire others in your singing of them.

Away in a Manger
(Cradle Song)

Anonymous (Verses 1 and 2)
John Thomas McFarland (Verse 3)

William J. Kirkpatrick
arranged by Christopher Ruck

pray. Bless all the dear ___ chil - dren in ___ your ten - der

care, and ___ fit us for heav - en, to ___ live with You

there. Be

near me Lord ___ Je - sus. ___

Coventry Carol

Robert Croo, d. 1534

English Melody
arranged by Joel K. Boyd

Moderately fast

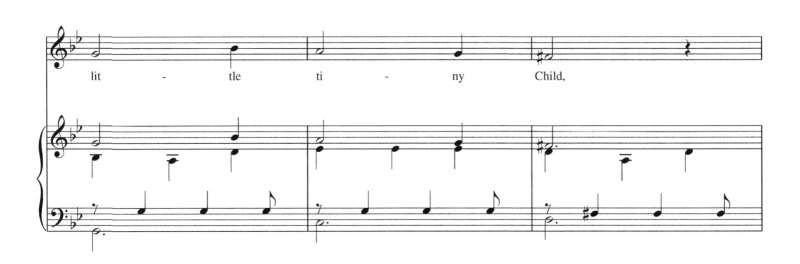

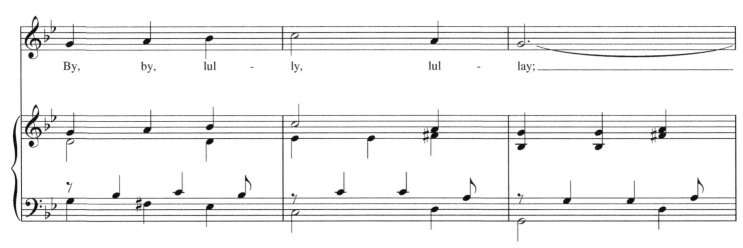

13

14

The First Noel

Traditional English Carol
arranged by Joel K. Boyd

sheep, on a cold win-ter's night ___ that was ___ so deep.

No - el ___ No - el, No - el, No - el!

Born is the King ___ of Is - ra - el!

mf

2. Then ___ let ___ us ___ all with ___ one ___ ac - cord sing ___

prais - es to _____ our heav - en - ly Lord;

That _ hath _____ made _ heav'n and _ earth _____ of

nought, and _ with _____ His blood _ man - kind _____ hath bought.

No - el, _____ No - el, No - el, No - el!

Good Christian Friends, Rejoice

Latin, 14th century
English words by John Mason Neale

"In dulci jubilo"
German Carol, 14th century
arranged by Richard Walters

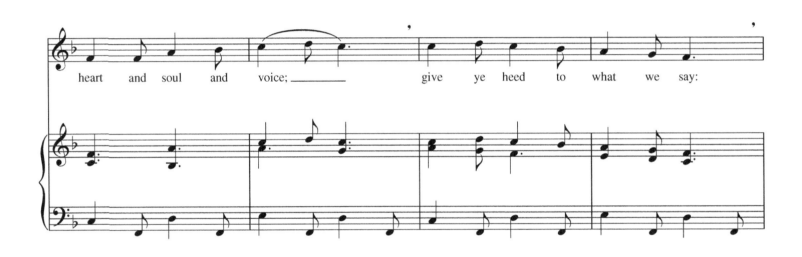

he is in the man - ger now. Christ is born to - day! _____

Christ is born to - day.

Good Chris - tian friends, re - joice _____ with

heart and soul and voice; _____ now ye hear of end - less bliss;

Je - sus Christ was born for this; he has o - pened

heav - ens door, we are blest for - ev - er - more. Christ was born for

this! _____ Christ was born for this!

mp Christ was born for this! _____ *mf* Christ was born for this!

In the Bleak Midwinter

Words by Christina Georgina Rossetti (1830–1894)

Music by Gustav Holst (1874–1934)
arranged by Brian Dean

snow_____ on_____ snow, in the bleak mid -

win - ter long,_____ long a - go.

What_____ can I give him,

poor_____ as I am? If I were a shep - herd,

He Is Born

18th century French Carol
arranged by Brian Dean

He is born, the div - ine Christ Child,

Play on the o - boe and bag - pipes mer - ri - ly!

He is born, the div - ine Christ Child,

Infant Holy, Infant Lowly

English text by Edith Margaret Gellibrand Reed

Polish Carol
arranged by Christopher Ruck

It Came upon the Midnight Clear

Edmund Hamilton Sears, 1849

Traditional English Melody
adapted by Arthur Sullivan
arranged by Richard Walters

It came up-on the mid-night clear, that glo-rious song of old, from an-gels bend-ing near the earth to touch their harps of gold. "Peace on the earth, good will to men, from

Joseph, Dearest Joseph Mine

14th century German Carol
arranged by Brian Dean

Gently rocking

"Jo - seph dear - est Jo - seph mine, help me cra - dle the Child di - vine. God re - ward thee and all that's thine in Pa - ra - dise," so prays the Vir - gin

O Come, Little Children

Christoph von Schmid, 1850

Johann Abraham Peter Schulz, 1850
arranged by Joel K. Boyd

hay and on straw; The shep - herds are kneel - ing be - fore Him in

awe. And Ma - ry and Jo - seph smile on Him with love, while

an - gels are sing - ing sweet songs from a - bove, while

an - gels are sing - ing sweet songs from a - bove.

O Come, O Come Emmanuel

Latin, 9th century
English words by John Mason Neale and Henry S. Coffin

French Melody, 15th century
arranged by Richard Walters

Once in Royal David's City

Mrs. Cecil Frances Alexander, 1848

Henry J. Gauntlett, 1849
arranged by Joel K. Boyd

Silent Night

Joseph Mohr

Franz Xaver Grüber
arranged by Christopher Ruck

Still, Still, Still

Traditional Austrian Carol
arranged by Brian Dean

Still, still, still, In a man-ger he lies in the chill. A-

round the Vir-gin an-gels are wing-ing, songs of joy-ous praise they are bring-ing.

Still, still, still, In a man-ger He lies in the chill.

Sussex Carol

Traditional English Carol
arranged by Christopher Ruck

Allegretto

On Christ - mas night all Chris - tians sing, To
why should we on earth be so sad, Since

hear the news __ the an - gels bring, On Christ - mas night all
our Re - deem - er made us glad, Then why should we on

Chris - tians sing, To hear the news ___ the an - gels bring.
earth be so sad, Since our Re - deem - er made us glad?

News of great joy ___ news of ___ great mirth,
When from our sin ___ He set ___ us free,

News of our bless - ed Sav - ior's birth.
All for to gain our lib - er -

Then ty? All

cresc.

f

54